The **RSPB Anthology** *of*
Wildlife Poetry

In loving memory of my father
Raymond Albert Barker
whose last words
were in praise of birds

First published 2011 by
A & C Black Publishers Ltd
an imprint of Bloomsbury Publishing Plc
49–51 Bedford Square, London, W1CB 3DP

www.acblack.com

Collection copyright © 2011 Celia Warren

The right of Celia Warren to be identified as the
compiler of this work has been asserted by her
in accordance with the Copyrights, Designs and Patents Act 1988.

ISBN 978-1-4081-3118-3

A CIP catalogue for this book is available from the British Library.

This book is produced using paper that is made from wood grown in
managed, sustainable forests. It is natural, renewable and recyclable.
The logging and manufacturing processes conform to the
environmental regulations of the country of origin.

Printed and bound in China by C&C Offset Printing Co., Ltd

The RSPB Anthology of Wildlife Poetry

SELECTED *by* CELIA WARREN

FOREWORD *by* ANDREW MOTION

A & C BLACK · LONDON

Foreword

My poem is set during a recent (2009) visit to the Lake District, and recalls a day I spent with my father as a child – a day I thought was going to be ordinary but turned out to be astonishing. An osprey! In my parent's world this was like seeing the Holy Grail, and of course this impressed me very much. But as I brooded later on what I had seen, I realised the sight had given me something other than astonishment. It had taught me that while rarity is marvellous, ordinary things are marvellous too – or can be if we look at them closely enough, and allow them to open our eyes to the connections that exist between all things.

This eye-opening is not simply allowed by poetry, but endlessly encouraged by it: as writers we are always trying to see things afresh, so that we can write about them in a fresh way. To 'make it new', as Ezra Pound said – but also to preserve the connections with things that are ancient and time-honoured.

In the same way that I tried to use my time as Poet Laureate to open people's minds to poetry, the RSPB aims to open people's eyes to nature. I'm happy to have written this poem to support their good cause. Perhaps there's a poem in this collection that will reflect an experience of your own?

Andrew Motion

As the Osprey to the Fish

Driving the length of England
we keep each other going with stories
of how it all began – in my own case
with my father abandoning the Spey
after a wet week of no salmon taking
to say: Tomorrow, Loch Garten; there
we'll see the only ospreys in Britain.

It was 1959 and I was seven – old enough
to know what bad luck meant: a boring
zig-zag across country towards the loch;
a panicky, slow sweep with binoculars;
and the nest like an upside-down wigwam
wedged in the balding pine, with not one
bird in sight, osprey or any other kind.

Back here in today, the evening light
survives as we enter the Lake District
and so, in the warmth of its last gasp,
we climb Loughrigg Fell for nothing more
than a bird's eye view of what survives:
smoke from the chimney of Dove Cottage
thinning over small roads and grey fields,

the marbled green lake thickening to black
as the breeze makes its cautious advances
and dies. Next minute the osprey slides in,
high and silent above our own high heads,
and neither of us find a word to say:
the sleek breast, the impassive golden eye,
the devastating cold beak are enough.

My own silence holds even when the wings,
with their mud fringe and chalky central panel,
labour hard enough for the downdraft to brush
the heart inside my body. Then I am lifted up
in the metal talons and ferried back to make
that sighting I missed with my father, although
no daylight remains as we leave the bare fell.

5

Contents

As the Osprey to the Fish   *Andrew Motion*   4

The First Day   *Phoebe Hesketh*   10

Haiku   *Alison Hunt*   12

Haiku   *J W Hackett*   13

I Wish I Was a Bird   *Roger Stevens*   14

Robin   *Iain Crichton Smith*   15

Broken Morning   *Moira Andrew*   16

The Dipper   *Kathleen Jamie*   17

Small, Smaller   *Russell Hoban*   18

Thaw   *Edward Thomas*   19

from Spring   *Christina Rossetti*   20

Pippa's Song   *Robert Browning*   21

Trees   *Sara Coleridge*   22

Loveliest of Trees   *A E Housman*   23

from Child's Song in Spring   *E Nesbit*   24

Web of Life   *Jane Clarke*   25

The Trees   *Graham Corcoran*   26

The Thrush's Nest   *John Clare*   28

Squirrel's the Word   *Sophie Hannah*   29

The Snail   *William Cowper*   30

Shell Villanelle   *Tony Mitton*   31

Nature Trail   *Benjamin Zephaniah*   32

Arion Ater Agg: The Black Slug   *Paul Hughes*   34

Mr Snail   *Celia Warren*   35

from The Ivy Green   *Charles Dickens*   36

Forest End   *Judith Nicholls*   37

Moor-Hens   *Charles Causley*   38

Ducks' Ditty   *Kenneth Grahame*   39

Down the Stream the Swans all Glide   *Spike Milligan*   40

Black Swan   *Graham Burchell*   41

The Bird at Dawn   *Harold Monro*   42

Ode by a Nightingale   *Rory Ewins*   43

Frog Hop   *John Agard*   44

Toad   *Norman MacCaig*   45

Tadpoles   *Peter Dixon*   46

The Very Fortunate Frog   *Chrissie Gittins*   47

Twenty Minute Walk   *Angela France*   48

City Bees   *Jennifer Curry*   49

Crow   *Roger Stevens*   50

A Tiding of Magpies   *Cornelia Davies*   51

The Windhover   *Gerard Manley Hopkins*   52

Cut Grass   *Philip Larkin*   53

The Gardener's Song   *Gareth Owen*   54

Hedgehog   *Liz Brownlee*   55

Mole   *Liz Brownlee*   56

Weasel   *Ted Hughes*   57

Brief Reflection on Cats Growing in Trees   *Miroslav Holub*   58

Old Foxy   *Sue Hardy-Dawson*   60

Night Prowler   *Jennifer Curry*   61

Jenny Wren   *Walter de la Mare*   62

A Bird came down the Walk   *Emily Dickinson*   63

Nothing Grows Old   *Phoebe Hesketh*   64

Home-Thoughts, from Abroad   *Robert Browning*   65

London Sparrows   *Philip Waddell*   66

Wren   *Celia Warren*   67

Gorse   *Gerard Benson*   68

Thistle   *Philip Waddell*   69

Short Measures   *Ben Jonson*   70

The Mayfly   *Andrew Collett*   70

Irony   *WH Hudson*   71

Ladette   *Alison Chisholm*   72

A Green Stink   *Gerard Benson*   73

Rush Hour   *Celia Warren*   74

No Hurry   *Eric Finney*   75

Worm's Eye View of the FA Cup Final   *Tony Mitton*   76

The Worth of Earthworms   *Tony Mitton*   77

Araneus Diadematus   *Gerard Benson*   78

Spinner   *Alison Brackenbury*   79

Foxgloves   *Jill Townsend*   80

The Blackberry   *Rory Ewins*   80

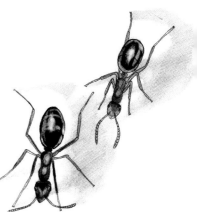

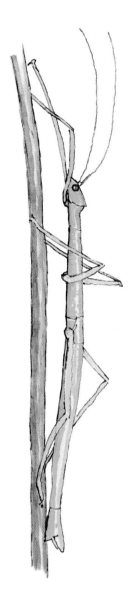

Conker   *Judith Nicholls*   81

The Fly   *William Blake*   82

All Creatures   *Gervase Phinn*   83

A Stick Insect   *Brian Moses*   84

Ladybird! Ladybird!   *Emily Brontë*   85

from Glanmore Eclogue   *Seamus Heaney*   86

To a Skylark   *Percy Bysshe Shelley*   87

Skylark   *Catherine Benson*   88

Up on the Downs   *Wes Magee*   89

Little Trotty Wagtail   *John Clare*   90

A Boy's Song   *James Hogg*   91

To the Cuckoo   *William Wordsworth*   92

Hopwas Hays Haiku   *Celia Warren*   94

Ella's Crane-Flies   *Fleur Adcock*   95

Seeing the Hare   *Catherine Benson*   96

Rabbits   *Graham Denton*   97

Slow Worm, Blind Worm, Legless Lizard   *Joan McLellan*   98

Aching Bones   *Debjani Chatterjee*   99

Sand Lizard   *Joan McLellan*   100

Young Adder   *Jill Townsend*   101

Creatures   *John Fuller*   102

Caterpillar   *Christina Rossetti*   103

The seven brains of a caterpillar   *Jan Dean*   104

Flying Crooked   *Robert Graves*   105

Don't Tread on Worms!   *Eric Finney*   106

The Good, the Bad and the Wriggly   *Jane A Russell*   107

The Dragon-fly   *Alfred, Lord Tennyson*   108

from To a Butterfly   *William Wordsworth*   109

There was an Old Man with a Beard   *Edward Lear*   110

There was an Old Man in a Tree   *Edward Lear*   110

Bee! I'm expecting you!   *Emily Dickinson*   111

A Cult Of Bees   *Philip Gross*   112

Ant Number 1,049,652   *Gerard Benson*   114

Earwig   *David Orme*   114

Woodlouse   *Judith Nicholls*   115

A Goldfinch   *Walter de la Mare*   117

Bullfinch   *Jan Dean*   117

Tall Nettles   *Edward Thomas*   118
On the Grasshopper and the Cricket   *John Keats*   119
River   *Rupert M Loydell*   120
Summer Paddling   *Coral Rumble*   121
Dancer   *Coral Rumble*   122
Salmon says …   *Celia Warren*   123
The Wild Swans at Coole   *WB Yeats*   124
The Eagle   *Alfred, Lord Tennyson*   126
Kestrel   *Ian Royce Chamberlain*   127
Crab   *Ted Hughes*   128
Nuffin' Like a Puffin   *John Rice*   129
(Unbridled) Guillemot   *John Hegley*   130
Bird Raptures   *Christina Rossetti*   132
Mushrooms   *Kenneth C Steven*   133
Proud Songsters   *Thomas Hardy*   134
Heron   *Angela Topping*   135
Take off   *Alison Brackenbury*   136
Bedtime   *Thomas Hood*   137
Shadow   *Michael Rosen*   138
The Centipede   *Ogden Nash*   139
The Firefly   *Anonymous*   139
Mice   *Rose Fyleman*   140
Field Mouse Sleeping   *James Carter*   141
Floating Harbour   *Helen Dunmore*   142
Blue Herons   *J Patrick Lewis*   143
Cliché   *Alison Chisholm*   144
Something Told the Wild Geese   *Rachel Field*   145
Bat   *Tony Mitton*   146
Bat Words   *Liz Brownlee*   147
The Owl   *Alfred, Lord Tennyson*   148
Night Hunter   *Sue Cowling*   149
Riddle   *Pie Corbett*   150
Badger   *Berlie Doherty*   151

Index of Titles   152
Acknowledgements   155

The First Day

The spotted fawn
Awoke in small leaf-netted suns
Tattooing him with coins where he lay
Beside his mother's warmth the first day
That gave him light,
The day that played him tunes
In water-music splashing over stones
And leaf-edged undertones
The day he learned the feel
Of dew on grass
Cool, cool and wet,
Of sun that steals the dew with sudden heat,
And heard the fret
In wind-turned willow leaves and wrinkled pool,
The day that filled his lungs with pollened wind
And smell of bracken, earth and dell-deep moss,
The day he came to know
Sharp hunger and the flow
Of milk to comfort his small emptiness,

The strangeness of his legs,
The bulwark of his mother's side,
The solace of her pink tongue's first caress,
Her snow-soft belly for his sheltering,
The rhythm of his needs
For movement and for rest,
For food and warmth and nest
Of flattened grass to fold himself in sleep.

Phoebe Hesketh

Haiku

Dappled sunlight on
blue and gold feathers – birds dance
around the peanuts.

Alison Hunt

Haiku

A bitter morning:
 sparrows sitting together
  without any necks.

J W Hackett

I Wish I Was a Bird

When the ice and frost and cold rains come
and from the north the howling gale
then
I wish I was a bird –

a swallow,

heading for Africa.
No ticket required,
no suitcase, no paraphernalia –

just me
and a wide open sky
and hundreds and thousands of cousins
all flying to the sun

Roger Stevens

Robin

If on a frosty morning
the robin redbreast calls
his waistcoat red and burning
like a beggar at your walls

throw breadcrumbs on the grass for him
when the ground is hard and still
for in his breast there is a flame
that winter cannot kill

Iain Crichton Smith

Broken Morning

A blackbird
scrapes
the lightening sky with knives of song,
wounds emptiness
with the lacerations
of its first
bleak notes.

The blackbird
sharpens
nightlong coldness
on a strop of frost,
whets loneliness
with its pale music
and I half-hear
a remembered voice.

Moira Andrew

The Dipper

It was winter, near freezing,
I'd walked through a forest of firs
when I saw issue out of the waterfall
a solitary bird.

It lit on a damp rock,
and, as water swept stupidly on,
wrung from its own throat
supple, undammable song.

It isn't mine to give.
I can't coax this bird to my hand
that knows the depth of the river
yet sings of it on land.

Kathleen Jamie

Small, Smaller

I thought that I knew all there was to know
Of being small, until I saw once, black against the snow
A shrew, trapped in my footprint, jump and fall
And jump again, and fall, the hole too deep, the walls too tall.

Russell Hoban

Thaw

Over the land freckled with snow half-thawed
The speculating rooks at their nests cawed
And saw from elm-tops, delicate as flower of grass,
What we below could not see, Winter pass.

Edward Thomas

from Spring

Frost-locked all the winter,
Seeds, and roots, and stones of fruits,
What shall make their sap ascend
That they may put forth shoots?
Tips of tender green,
Leaf, or blade, or sheath;
Telling of the hidden life
That breaks forth underneath,
Life nursed in its grave by Death.

Blows the thaw-wind pleasantly,
Drips the soaking rain,
By fits looks down the waking sun:
Young grass springs on the plain;
Young leaves clothe early hedgerow trees;
Seeds, and roots, and stones of fruits,
Swollen with sap put forth their shoots;
Curled-headed ferns sprout in the lane;
Birds sing and pair again.

Christina Rossetti

Pippa's Song

The year's at the spring,
And day's at the morn;
Morning's at seven;
The hillside dew-pearled;
The lark's on the wing;
The snail's on the thorn;
God's in his heaven –
All's right with the world!

Robert Browning

Trees

The Oak is called the King of Trees,
The Aspen quivers in the breeze,
The Poplar grows up straight and tall,
The Pear tree spreads along the wall,
The Sycamore gives pleasant shade,
The Willow droops in watery glade,
The Fir tree useful timber gives,
The Beech amid the forest lives.

Sara Coleridge

Loveliest of Trees

Loveliest of trees, the cherry now
Is hung with bloom along the bough,
And stands about the woodland ride
Wearing white for Eastertide.

Now, of my threescore years and ten,
Twenty will not come again,
And take from seventy springs a score
It only leaves me fifty more.

And since to look at things in bloom
Fifty springs are little room,
About the woodlands I will go
To see the cherry hung with snow.

A E Housman

from Child's Song in Spring

The silver birch is a dainty lady,
    She wears a satin gown;
The elm tree makes the churchyard shady,
    She will not live in town.

The English oak is a sturdy fellow;
    He gets his green coat late;
The willow is smart in a suit of yellow,
    While brown the beech trees wait.

The chestnut's proud, and the lilac's pretty,
    The poplar's gentle and tall,
But the plane tree's kind to the poor dull city –
    I love him best of all!

E Nesbit

Web of Life

An invisible web,
as fragile as dreams,
links mountains to valleys
and rivers to streams,

Through woodlands and forest;
where seas flow and ebb,
over ice caps and deserts,
life weaves a great web.

From plankton to whales,
all life great and small
depends on each other.
Life's web links us all.

And we must take care
of each gossamer thread,
for we are all part of
this great world wide web.

Jane Clarke

The Trees

Down at Casey Avenue
They'd come to chop the trees;
There were seven healthy birches to be felled.
I couldn't bear to watch them
So I marched across the street:
"I think there must be some mistake!" I yelled.

The man turned off his chainsaw,
Then he grinned and shook his head:
"It's council orders, matey," he replied.
"They're causing an obstruction
So it's time for them to go,
I'd be grateful if you'd kindly step aside."

I flopped against the tree trunk
Which was more an ageing friend,
As it stretched across the tarmac, proud and high.
I'd known it as a sapling
When the kids were still at school,
And was finding it a struggle not to cry.

26

An obstruction? Was he kidding?
No, I wouldn't step aside!
Those handsome trees were nothing of the sort.
Doors began to open
And I almost gave a cheer
As my neighbours came to offer their support.

They were more than trees, we argued,
They were more than leaves and branches,
They were part of how we felt and what we were.
Maturing, just as we had,
In their own determined way.
So how could such an awful thing occur?

He listened...then he nodded,
We were almost home and dry,
Then he grinned again, and turned the saw back on!
Those trees were shade and privacy,
Those trees were life itself,
But they got in someone's way...and now they're gone!

Graham Corcoran

The Thrush's Nest

Within a thick and spreading hawthorn bush
That overhung a molehill large and round,
I heard from morn to morn a merry thrush
Sing hymns to sunrise, and I drank the sound
With joy; and often, an intruding guest,
I watched her secret toil from day to day –
How true she warped the moss to form a nest,
And modelled it within with wood and clay;
And by and by, like heath-bells gilt with dew,
There lay her shining eggs, as bright as flowers,
Ink-spotted over shells of greeny blue;
And there I witnessed, in the sunny hours,
A brood of nature's minstrels chirp and fly,
Glad as the sunshine and the laughing sky.

John Clare

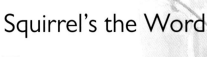

Squirrel's the Word

They're rats with bushy tails, you claim.
They bite and spread disease.
Despite the reassuring name
Of squirrel, they are wild, not tame,
And they belong in trees.

But there's a squirrel that I know
Who calls each day at nine,
Catches the croissant that I throw
And chomps it on the patio.
I think of him as mine.

He is both patient and polite
While I prepare his meal.
Squirrel's the word and it's the right
Word in his case, in fact he's quite
The squirrelish ideal,

So deconstruct him all you please
To bushy tail and rat.
Squirrel is still the name for these
Creatures with squirrels' qualities
And he is just like that.

Sophie Hannah

The Snail

To grass, or leaf, or fruit, or wall,
The snail sticks close, nor fears to fall,
As if he grew there, house and all
Together.

Within that house secure he hides,
When danger imminent betides
Of storm, or other harm besides
Of weather.

Give but his horns the slightest touch,
His self-collecting power is such
He shrinks into his house with much
Displeasure.

Where'er he dwells, he dwells alone,
Except himself has chattels none,
Well satisfied to be his own
Whole treasure.

Thus hermit-like, his life he leads,
Nor partner of his banquet needs,
And if he meets one only feeds
The faster.

Who seeks him must be worse than blind,
(He and his house are so combined,)
If, finding it, he fails to find
Its master.

William Cowper

Shell Villanelle

I am a snail. This shell is where I hide.
The world is full of danger, threat and spite.
My brittle canopy feels safe inside.

My way is slow. A snail's pace I slide.
I have no speed, no means of sudden flight.
I am a snail. This shell is where I hide.

With steady caution through the world I glide.
If shadows loom, or things flash fast and bright,
my brittle canopy feels safe inside.

I cannot parry stabbing beaks with pride,
nor wear my armour like a valiant knight.
I am a snail. This shell is where I hide.

If jabbing birds should come, all glitter-eyed,
I have no way to stand at bay and fight.
My brittle canopy feels safe inside.

But for this case, I'd long ago have died.
And so this spell I steadily recite:
I am a snail. This shell is where I hide.
My brittle canopy feels safe inside.

Tony Mitton

31

Nature Trail

At the bottom of my garden
There's a hedgehog and a frog
And a lot of creepy-crawlies
Living underneath a log,
There's a baby daddy long legs
And an easy-going snail
And a family of woodlice,
All are on my nature trail.

There are caterpillars waiting
For their time to come to fly,
There are worms turning the earth over
As ladybirds fly by,
Birds will visit, cats will visit
But they always choose their time
And I've even seen a fox visit
This wild garden of mine.

Squirrels come to nick my nuts
And busy bees come buzzing
And when the night time comes
Sometimes some dragonflies come humming,
My garden mice are very shy
And I've seen bats that growl
And in my garden I have seen
A very wise old owl.

My garden is a lively place
There's always something happening,
There's this constant search for food
And then there's all that flowering,
When you have a garden
You will never be alone
And I believe we all deserve
A garden of our own.

Benjamin Zephaniah

Arion Ater Agg: The Black Slug

Twenty-seven thousand teeth,
no shell above but slime beneath,
their appetite's beyond belief,
they eat their weight each day.
And if you grow azaleas
or try your hand at dahlias,
you'll soon grow used to failure,
they'll munch your blooms away.
It doesn't matter what you do,
they'll always get one up on you.
They'll crunch on leaves the whole night through
and strip your garden bare.
And even if you spend the night
with salt and spade, prepared to fight,
they'll wipe the floor with you, all right,
you haven't got a prayer.
Don't be upset, don't look forlorn,
abandon beds and plant a lawn;
you'll never have to dread the dawn,
for slugs don't dine on grass.
They'll soon give up and move next door,
though mowing lawns can be a bore
you'll stay slug-free, forever more
and sleep, in peace, at last.

Paul Hughes

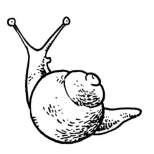
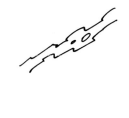

Mr Snail

Quaint and quirky, never quick,
Mother Nature's glue-stick,
Hard shell, tacky tail,
Glue the garden, Mister Snail.

Celia Warren

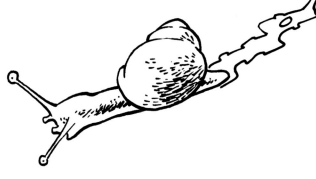

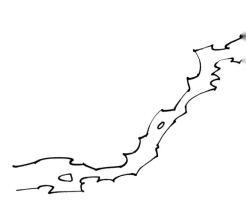

from The Ivy Green

Whole ages have fled and their works decayed,
  And nations have scattered been;
But the stout old Ivy shall never fade,
  From its hale and hearty green.
The brave old plant, in its lonely days,
  Shall fatten upon the past:
For the stateliest building man can raise
  Is the Ivy's food at last.
          Creeping on where time has been,
          A rare old plant is the Ivy green.

Charles Dickens

Forest End

Since they left the house
the trees moved in;
the oak and ash made a home.
Where the chimney stood
is a jagged pine,
and the roof has almost gone.

Since they left the house
the birds moved in;
you can hear the thrush's song.
The house awakes
to the squawk of rooks,
and sleeps when the owl has flown.

Since they left the house
the winds moved in;
the windows wail and groan.
A few stairs creak
to a clouded sky,
then the house is left, alone.

Judith Nicholls

Moor-Hens

Living by Bate's Pond, they
(Each spring and summer day)
Watched among reed and frond
The moor-hens prank and play.

Watched them dip and dive,
Watched them pass, re-pass,
Spluttering over the water
As if it were made of glass.

Watched them gallop the mud
Bobbing a tail, a head;
Under an April stream
Swimming with tails outspread.

Listened at night for a cry
Striking the sky like a stone;
The kik! kik! of farewell
As they drifted south for the sun.

Whose are the children, and who
Are the children who lived by the pond,
Summer and spring year-long
When the wild sun shone?
Thirsty the stream, and dry;
Ah, and the house is gone.

Charles Causley

Ducks' Ditty

All along the backwater,
Through the rushes tall,
Ducks are a-dabbling,
Up tails all!

Ducks' tails, drakes' tails,
Yellow feet a-quiver,
Yellow bills all out of sight
Busy in the river!

Slushy green undergrowth
Where the roach swim –
Here we keep our larder,
Cool and full and dim.

Everyone for what he likes!
We like to be
Heads down, tails up,
Dabbling free!

High in the blue above
Swifts whirl and call –
We are down a-dabbling,
Up tails all!

Kenneth Grahame

Down the Stream the Swans all Glide

Down the stream the swans all glide;
It's quite the cheapest way to ride.
Their legs get wet,
Their tummies wetter:
I think after all
The bus is better.

Spike Milligan

Bewicks Swans.
Slimbridge 31 1 01

Black Swan

On one leg
I feel the deep-earth cool,
the slide of an inch of water
before it drops, white in sun sparks,
and I swan-dream of a summer
of days like this; my hard red mouth
in the down of my feathers, black
as anthracite gathering heat
from a distant star.

Graham Burchell

The Bird at Dawn

What I saw was just one eye
In the dawn as I was going:
A bird can carry all the sky
In that little button glowing.

Never in my life I went
So deep into a firmament.

He was standing on a tree,
All in blossom overflowing;
And purposely looked hard at me,
At first, as if to question merrily:
"Where are you going?"
But next some far more serious thing to say:
I could not answer, could not look away.

Oh, that hard, round, and so distracting eye:
Little mirror of the sky! –
And then the after-song another tree
Held, and sent radiating back on me.

If no man had invented human word,
And a bird-song had been
The only way to utter what we mean,
What would we men have heard,
What understood, what seen,
Between the trills and pauses, in between
The singing and the silence of a bird?

Harold Monro

Ode by a Nightingale

Give me birdsong: so subtle, so sweet!
So expressive, with such a fair beat!
Who could ever forget
That divine minuet,
"Tweet Tweet Tweet Tweet Tweet Tweet Tweet Tweet Tweet"?

Rory Ewins

Frog Hop

I may be ugly
but I have my hop.

I have no wish
to be kissed
and turned
to a prince
and mince
along
in awkward
finery.

Me? Abandon
my kingdom
of wet and weed
and insect feast?

Oh keep your kiss.
Oh keep your prince
dressed like a fop.

I'll keep my hop.

John Agard

Toad

Stop looking like a purse. How could a purse
squeeze under the rickety door and sit,
full of satisfaction, in a man's house?

You clamber towards me on your four corners –
right hand, left foot, left hand, right foot.

I love you for being a toad,
for crawling like a Japanese wrestler,
and for not being frightened.

I put you in my purse hand, not shutting it,
and set you down outside directly under
every star.

A jewel in your head? Toad,
you've put one in mine,
a tiny radiance in a dark place.

Norman MacCaig

45

Tadpoles

Said the tadpole to the tadpole
as they tadpoled round their jar
I don't want to be a froggy
I don't want to grow that far.
I'm happy as I am now
black blob and little tail,
I don't want to be a froggy
or a toady
or a whale.

I just want to be a taddy
I want to stay the same
I liked being frogspawn
I didn't want to change …
Oh, why've I got to grow up
and be an ugly toad,
creep around in ditches
– and get squashed in the road?
I'd like to stay a taddy,
stay the same for life.
This jar can be my palace …

and you can be my wife.

Peter Dixon

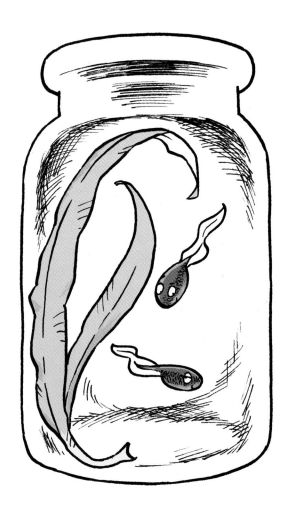

The Very Fortunate Frog

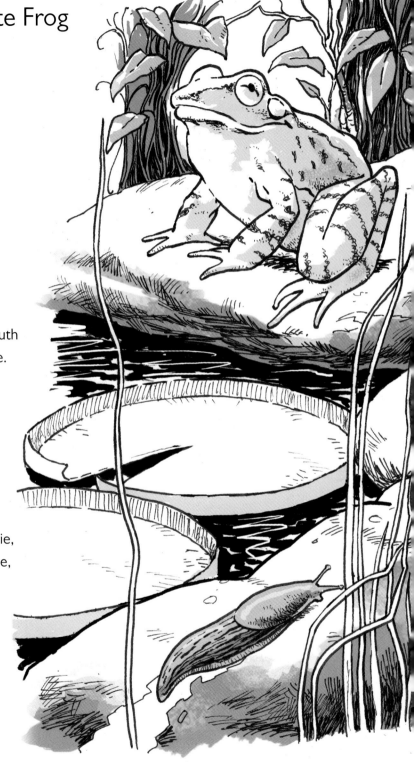

I live in a rubber tub,
it's a very fancy home,
my ceiling's made of lily pads,
I really cannot moan.

At night I go for a wander,
slurp up a worm or two,
flick on a fly, and wonder why
some frogs live in a zoo.

For pudding I like a slug,
slimy and black as coal,
I lick my lips and open my mouth
and swallow my captive whole.

I plan on living for forty years,
squelching in the mud,
basking in the morning sun,
if I could dance a jig I would.

On hot days in July,
when I'm feeling sleepy-snoozie,
a hose pipe fills my fancy home,
and turns it into a jacuzzi.

Chrissie Gittins

Twenty Minute Walk

a little more than twenty minutes,
if you take the path through the old cutting.
Turn into the lane where the fence bulges
with the sprawl of ivy and viburnum, where
tree-roots push steel posts to drunken leaning.
Before you go through the gap by the bridge,
allow yourself a minute to rest your hands
on the parapet, to look down on the space
once ruled by cold iron; see how relentless
are blackthorn and nettle in the blur of straight lines.
There is always a wet patch at that gap, take care
not to get stuck in noticing how bent and trodden
grass persists through puddled mud.
The steps cut into the bank can be slippery. Go slow
so that you can hear the traffic noise fade
as if you're stepping into deep water:
long grass waves like kelp fronds, the air filters green.
You'll need two minutes to stop at the blackbird's warning,
to watch a wren flutter through the shabby tangle of hawthorn.
Follow the line of the cutting to the end
where the blinded tunnel holds stories of the lost
in the sooty smears on the wall, the empty bottles.
Climb the path by the tunnel, turn back to the road
next to the house smothered in wisteria: you'll want
some time to measure what is hidden
in its folds and tangles. Don't lose yourself
in its twists.

Angela France

City Bees

In a drab back yard
At the back of his shop
Among boxes and bins
A world away
From flowering fields
And hedgerows in blossom
Mr Patel keeps bees.

City bees.
They browse on buddleia and
Ragged weeds
Rosebay willowherb
And dust-heavy trees
But their busy wings
Bring sweetness
To the city.

Jennifer Curry

49

Crow

Crow sits in the March branches
Of a rail-side tree
Beside the black scribble
Of last year's nest
Planning this year's
offensive

Roger Stevens

A Tiding of Magpies

One for sorrow lands gracefully, gliding:
A second one, joyful, from hiding –
Now six magpies scold,
Which could mean there'll be gold –
There's a bunch of them … must be a tiding.

Cornelia Davies

The Windhover

I caught this morning morning's minion, king-
  dom of daylight's dauphin, dapple-dawn-drawn Falcon, in his riding
  Of the rolling level underneath him steady air, and striding
High there, how he rung upon the rein of a wimpling wing
In his ecstasy! then off, off forth on swing,
  As a skate's heel sweeps smooth on a bow-bend: the hurl and gliding
  Rebuffed the big wind. My heart in hiding
Stirred for a bird, – the achieve of; the mastery of the thing!

Brute beauty and valour and act, oh, air, pride, plume, here
  Buckle! And the fire that breaks from thee then, a billion
Times told lovelier, more dangerous, O my chevalier!

  No wonder of it: sheer plod makes plough down sillion
Shine, and blue-bleak embers, ah my dear,
  Fall, gall themselves, and gash gold-vermillion.

Gerard Manley Hopkins

Cut Grass

Cut grass lies frail:
Brief is the breath
Mown stalks exhale.
Long, long the death.

It dies in the white hours
Of young-leafed June
With chestnut flowers,
With hedges snowlike strewn,

White lilac bowed,
Lost lanes of Queen Anne's lace,
And that high-builded cloud
Moving at summer's pace.

Philip Larkin

The Gardener's Song

Look, here he come a-visiting
My bristle brush, my mate,
Up from the privet hedge
To my breakfast plate.
Here he come a-trundling
On his jacked-up legs,
Past our Megan's washing
And the string bag full of pegs.
And I'm glad to see thee Mister,
Good morning to you,
With your hunched back full of arrows
And your nose in the dew.
Don't need no invitation
To pleasure my eye,
Come up and see me any time
My hedgehog Samurai.

Gareth Owen

Hedgehog

A hedgehog's hug is mainly hid
beneath its sharp and spiky lid,
and when it rolls into a ball
a hedgehog has no hug at all.

Liz Brownlee

Mole

Under the grass,
and in the loam,
is where I make
my tunnel home.

I push out soil
with spade paws, till
I have enough
to make a hill.

I live alone,
on worms I dine,
earth is my life —
it's mine, all mine!

Liz Brownlee

Weasel

The Weasel whizzes through the woods, he sizzles through the brambles,
Compared to him a rabbit hobbles and a whippet ambles.

He's all the heads of here and there, he spins you in a dither,
He's peering out of everywhere, his ten tails hither thither.

The Weasel never waits to wonder what it is he's after.
It's butchery he wants, and BLOOD, and merry belly laughter.

That's all, that's all, it's no good thinking he's a darling creature.
Weight for weight, he's twice a tiger, which he'd like to teach you.

A lucky thing we're giants! It can't be very nice
Dodging from the Weasel down the mazes of the mice.

Ted Hughes

Brief Reflection on
Cats Growing in Trees

When moles still had their annual general meetings
and when they still had better eyesight it befell
that they expressed a wish to discover what was above.

So they elected a commission to ascertain what was above.
The commission dispatched a sharp-sighted fleet-footed
mole. He, having left his native mother earth,
caught sight of a tree with a bird on it.

Thus a theory was put forward that up above
birds grew on trees. However,
some moles thought this was
too simple. So they dispatched another
mole to ascertain if birds did grow on trees.

By then it was evening and on the tree
some cats were mewing. Mewing cats,
the second mole announced, grew on the tree.
Thus an alternative theory emerged about cats.

The two conflicting theories bothered an elderly
neurotic member of the commission. And he
climbed up to see for himself.
By then it was night and all was pitch-black.

Both schools are mistaken, the venerable mole declared.
Birds and cats are optical illusions produced
by the refraction of light. In fact, things above

Were the same as below, only the clay was less dense and
the upper roots of the trees were whispering something,
but only a little.

And that was that.

Ever since the moles have remained below ground:
they do not set up commissions
or presuppose the existence of cats.

Or if so only a little.

Miroslav Holub

Old Foxy

The
urban
fox waits for Monday night's
feast, of Sunday's roast chicken bones
jellied and greased. Lunch in
the lamplight. Fish heads
with leeks, crisp
rinds of
bacon
and pizza
midweek.
Brave bin
buccaneer,
Midnight's
dark thief, of
pitas with curry
smoked ham or
corned beef. So
while the house
dozes and Heel-
Nipper sleeps, Old
Foxy hunts hedges
then craftily creeps,
up on packed lunches,
down wild city streets,
for the cold fatty flavours
of half-eaten treats.
Then
with
sliced
mutton
sliver and
sausage for
sweet, slinks
back in the
shadows, to
his grand
country
seat.

Sue Hardy-Dawson

Night Prowler

Skulking round the dustbins,
Flame-red in dead of night,
Sharp-pricked ears, dark plume of a tail –
Urban fox on the backstreet trail.

Jennifer Curry

Jenny Wren

Of all the birds that rove and sing,
  Near dwellings made for men,
None is so nimble, feat, and trim
As Jenny Wren.

With pin-point bill, and tail a-cock,
  So wildly shrill she cries,
The echoes on their roof-tree knock
And fill the skies.

Never was sweeter seraph hid
  Within so small a house –
A tiny, inch-long, eager, ardent,
Feathered mouse.

Walter de la Mare

A Bird came down the Walk

A Bird came down the Walk—
He did not know I saw—
He bit an angle-worm in halves
And ate the fellow, raw,

And then he drank a Dew
From a convenient Grass,
And then hopped sidewise to the Wall
To let a Beetle pass—

He glanced with rapid eyes
That hurried all abroad—
They looked like frightened Beads, I thought—
He stirred his velvet head

Like one in danger, Cautious,
I offered him a Crumb,
And he unrolled his feathers
And rowed him softer home—

Than Oars divide the Ocean,
Too silver for a seam—
Or Butterflies, off Banks of Noon,
Leap, plashless as they swim.

Emily Dickinson

Nothing Grows Old

This is the hour the gods set to music:
Song in the branches, hope in the heart,
Rhythm in poplars like green spires adorning
The morning in tune with the moment apart.

Today is a soaring; and summit and steeple
And smoke from the clearing discover the sky.
Uncover the sky for us, upward-bound-skylark –
The song will remain though the singer must die.

This is the peak of the measureless minute
That mankind aspires to and never can hold,
Disclosed in a flash by a primrose, a linnet –
The instant that tells us that nothing grows old.

Phoebe Hesketh

Home-Thoughts, from Abroad

Oh, to be in England
Now that April's there,
And whoever wakes in England
Sees, some morning, unaware,
That the lowest boughs and the brushwood sheaf
Round the elm-tree bole are in tiny leaf,
While the chaffinch sings on the orchard bough
In England – now!

And after April, when May follows,
And the whitethroat builds, and all the swallows –
Hark! where my blossomed pear-tree in the hedge
Leans to the field and scatters on the clover
Blossoms and dewdrops – at the bent spray's edge –
That's the wise thrush; he sings his song twice over
Lest you should think he never could recapture
The first fine careless rapture!
And though the fields look rough with hoary dew,
All will be gay when noontide wakes anew
The buttercups, the little children's dower
– Far brighter than this gaudy melon flower!

Robert Browning

London Sparrows

House sparrows down
In London town
Must do their best
To build a nest.

A lock of hair
From Soho Square,
A satin bow
From Pimlico.

A dead shoelace
From Portland Place,
A millet stalk
From Birdcage Walk.

A rubber band
Found in The Strand,
Some tired old moss
From Charing Cross.

Some bits of rag
And plastic bag
Tugged from a bin
At Lincoln's Inn.

A used bus pass,
Some twigs and grass
And willow bark…?
St James' Park!

Philip Waddell

Wren

Farthing-framed I found you, first,
when, as a child, I clutched the coin
possessing you, wren.

Flimsy-feathered, as small and round
as the coin you graced, caught in a glimpse,
capricious wren.

Warming the woods with your warning trill,
you burrow in bracken and bramble,
warbling wren.

Stolen from skies to thrill the earth,
a tilt-tail joker, bewildering winter,
whimsical wren.

Celia Warren

Gorse

Gorse is a trumpet song,
　It spikes out of the earth,
　　A welcome pain.

It will spear your hands,
　It will wound your skin,
　　Bead you with scarlet.

It is "I am" in all seasons.
　It blares its trumpet song,
　　Tan-ta-ra to the skies.

It is a still fire.
　Yellow on the hillsides,
　　Coldly burning.

Gerard Benson

Thistle

You're a punk of a plant; like a troublesome teen
You loiter and idle and try to look mean:
You're a rogue and a Romeo sowing your seed —
Well, I'd think it foolish to call you a weed!

You've that look, says to me, you don't care what I think
As on the embankment you sunbathe and drink:
With Bramble and Nettle and Hogweed and Sloe
You were born to be wild on the edge of Skid Row.

You're one of those plants seems to thrive on neglect,
You're a bighead, a show-off from which I'd expect
If you laughed it would be with an insolent bray
To go with your cocky, rebellious way.

Philip Waddell

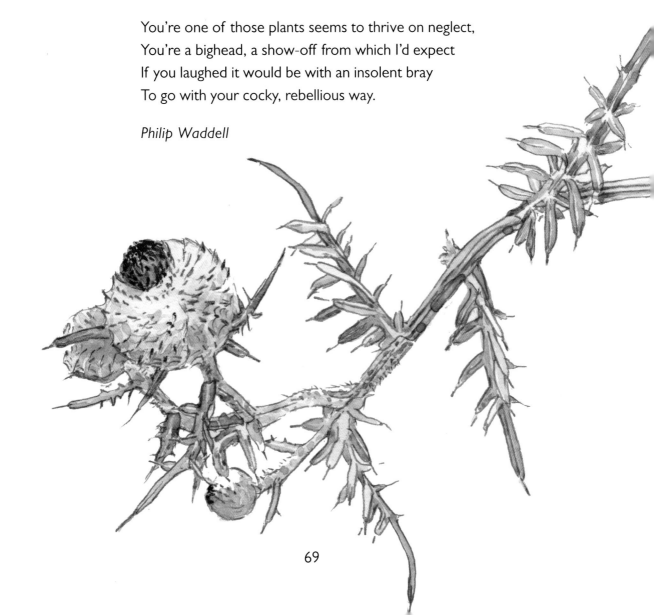

Short Measures

It is not growing like a tree
In bulk, doth make man better be,
Or standing long an oak, three hundred year,
To fall a log at last, dry, bald, and sear:
A lily of the day
Is fairer far in May
Although it fall and die that night;
It was the plant, the flower of light.
In small proportions we just beauties see,
And in short measures life may perfect be.

Ben Jonson

The Mayfly

A mayfly's ambition
isn't to run with the wind
or to try and get her own way.

A mayfly's ambition
is simply to be able
to live for more than one day.

Andrew Collett

Irony

It stood a hundred years, a lonely giant,
Mid summer lightnings, winter storms, defiant.
One hush'd night came a crash; and morning found
The proud tree stretch'd in ruin on the ground.

WH Hudson

71

Ladette

Beneath a holly tree,
grass cool, a dandelion
shocks the garden's ordered elegance.
Brash gold sticks out its tongue
at rollered lawns, flirts in the breeze,
raises its skirts to flash green petticoats.
Plucked, it starts to darken,
rage fuelling impudence,
outer petals down-turned, petulant,
amber mop at the centre bristling.

If it could speak
it would shout *knickers*.

Alison Chisholm

A Green Stink

A green stink where the root
lies oozing on the bonfire heap.

Water spreads over the low meadows
after a month of rain, and a heron

stands still as a thorn bush. "Wet
the bed. Wet the bed!" The child,

her fingers milk-sticky where she peeled
the stem, blows seeds and time

into this April morning. Young leaves
to cull and wash for a salad.

And all over the field, aggressive
little suns, yellow without compromise.

Gerard Benson

Rush Hour

Sparrows spit their tunes
through petrol fumes and rumbling
early morning rush.

Celia Warren

74

No Hurry

On the motorway banks
As we speed past,
Airily waving,
Whitely massed:
Moon daisies,
Calm and lovely-faced,
Silently asking,
"Why such haste?"

Eric Finney

75

Worm's Eye View of the FA Cup Final

"That's funny," said the worm
as it went under Wembley.
"I wonder why the ground's
so loud and trembly."

Tony Mitton

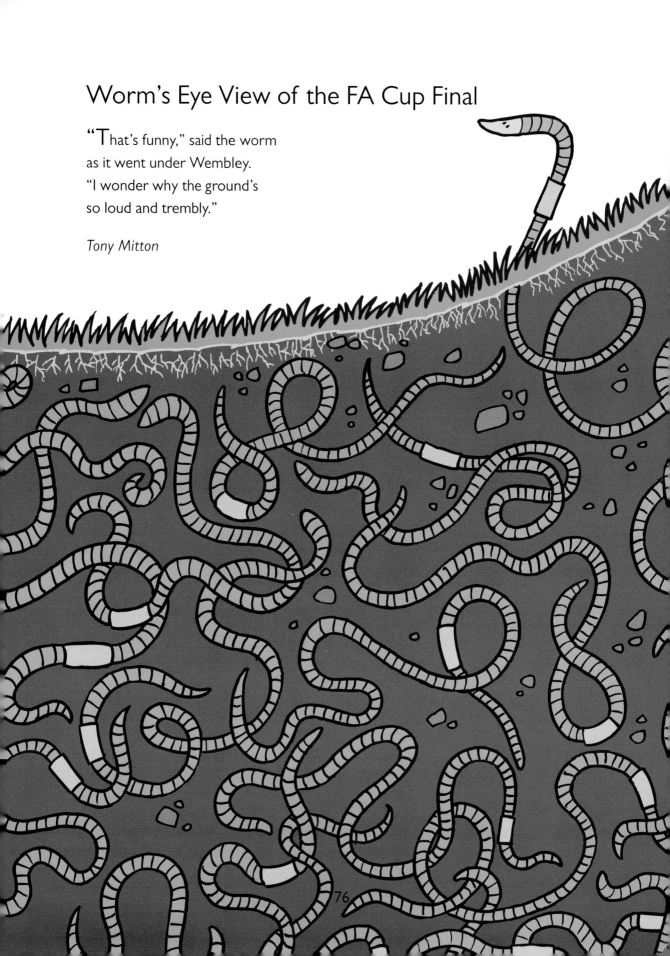

76

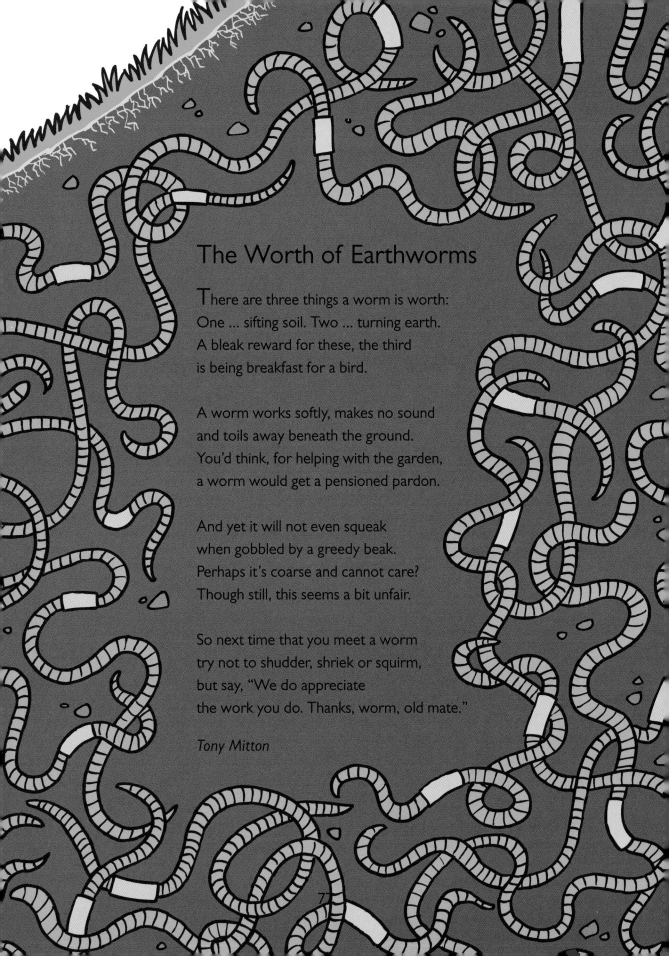

The Worth of Earthworms

There are three things a worm is worth:
One ... sifting soil. Two ... turning earth.
A bleak reward for these, the third
is being breakfast for a bird.

A worm works softly, makes no sound
and toils away beneath the ground.
You'd think, for helping with the garden,
a worm would get a pensioned pardon.

And yet it will not even squeak
when gobbled by a greedy beak.
Perhaps it's coarse and cannot care?
Though still, this seems a bit unfair.

So next time that you meet a worm
try not to shudder, shriek or squirm,
but say, "We do appreciate
the work you do. Thanks, worm, old mate."

Tony Mitton

Araneus Diadematus

Agile I am, a high-wire walker.
A skilful ropemaker.
I can abseil downward
Or climb improbably through the air.

I'm a patient waiter,
A swift runner, a heartless poisoner,
An architect of fantastic geometries,
A complicated dancer.

There are some who fear me
Among the fleshy bipeds,
My plump body scares them,
My eight angle-poised legs.

Or perhaps it's an idea
That fills them with terror –
That I may have a mind,
That I, too, have a maker.

Gerard Benson

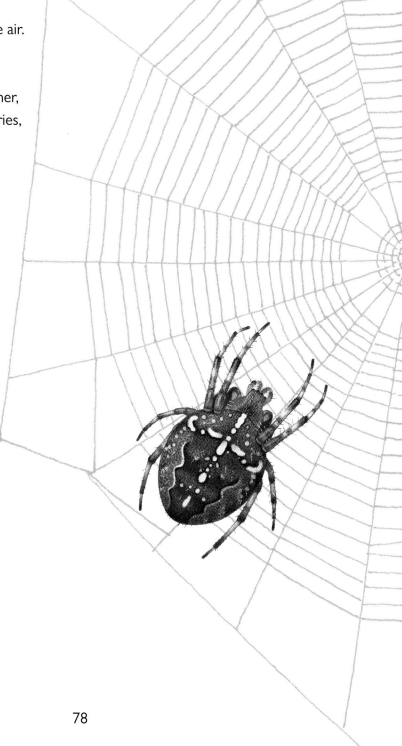

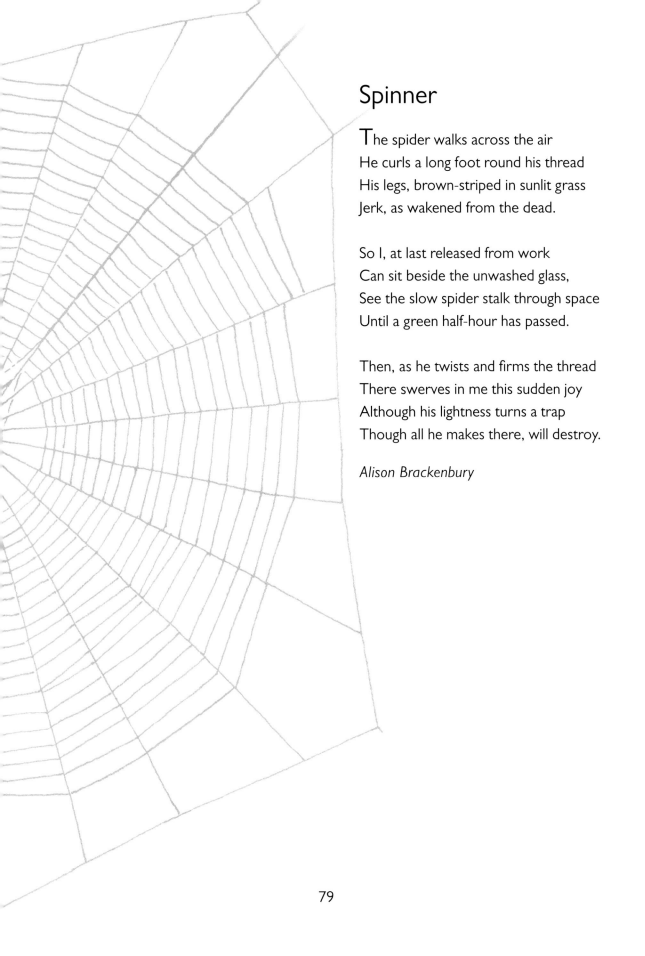

Spinner

The spider walks across the air
He curls a long foot round his thread
His legs, brown-striped in sunlit grass
Jerk, as wakened from the dead.

So I, at last released from work
Can sit beside the unwashed glass,
See the slow spider stalk through space
Until a green half-hour has passed.

Then, as he twists and firms the thread
There swerves in me this sudden joy
Although his lightness turns a trap
Though all he makes there, will destroy.

Alison Brackenbury

Foxgloves

Purple spires
that bees like boys
climb inside
and fill with noise.

Jill Townsend

The Blackberry

The blackberry grows in a thicket
Of thorns – any finger, they'll prick it –
But tastes so inviting
I long to start biting,
And scramble through brambles to pick it.

Rory Ewins

Conker

Take care!
Inside my hedgehog-shell,
sharp as a warrior's shield,
a small case, leather-polished;
inside the polished case,
silent, unsuspected ...

secret spells!

Spells for making
candles of cream lace
to light the waiting spring;
giant arms, high-reaching,
to cobweb for ever
against winter skies;
leaves, fine-fanned
to scatter sunlight
over summer grass ...

and more like me
to catch the eyes of passers-by
like newly-bronzed stained glass.

Judith Nicholls

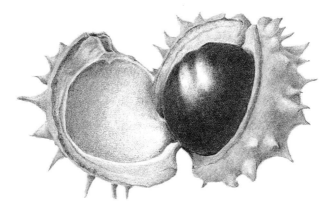

The Fly

Little fly
Thy summer's play
My thoughtless hand
Has brushed away.

Am not I
A fly like thee?
Or art not thou
A man like me?

For I dance
And drink and sing
Till some blind hand
Shall brush my wing.

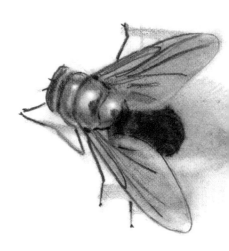

If thought is life
And strength and breath
And the want
Of thought is death

Then am I
A happy fly,
If I live,
Or if I die.

William Blake

All Creatures

I just can't seem to help it,
I love creatures – great and small,
But it's the ones that others do not like
I love the best of all.
I like creepy-crawly beetles
And shiny black-backed bugs,
Gnats and bats and spiders,
And slimy fat black slugs.
I like chirpy little crickets
And buzzing bumblebees,
Lice and mice and ladybirds,
And tiny jumping fleas.
I like wasps and ants and locusts,
Centipedes and snails,
Moles and voles and earwigs
And rats with long pink tails.
I like giant moths with dusty wings
And maggots fat and white,
Worms and germs and weevils,
And fireflies in the night.
No, I just can't seem to help it,
To me not one's a pest,
It's the ones that others do not like,
I seem to love the best.
So it makes it rather difficult,
It's enough to make me cry,
Because my job's in pest control,
And I just couldn't hurt a fly.

Gervase Phinn

A Stick Insect

A stick insect
is not a thick insect,
a macho-built-like-a-brick insect,
a brawl-and-break-it-up-quick insect,
not a sleek-and-slippery-slick insect
or a hold-out-your-hand-for-a-lick insect.

No way could you say it's a cuddly pet
or a butterfly that hasn't happened yet.

And it won't come running when you call
or chase about after a ball.
And you can't take it out for a walk
or try and teach it how to talk.

It's a hey-come-and-look-at-this-quick insect,
a how-can-you-tell-if-it's-sick insect,
a don't-mistake-me-for-a-stick
          insect...

Brian Moses

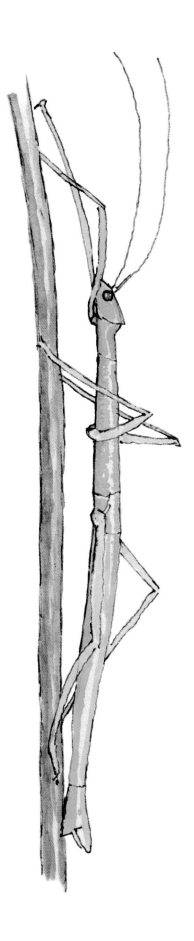

Ladybird! Ladybird!

Ladybird! Ladybird! Fly away home,
Night is approaching, and sunset is come:
The herons are flown to their trees by the Hall;
Felt, but unseen, the damp dewdrops fall.
This is the close of a still summer day;
Ladybird! Ladybird! Haste! Fly away!

Emily Brontë

from Glanmore Eclogue

Early summer, cuckoo cuckoos,
Welcome, summer is what he sings.
Heather breathes on soft bog-pillows.
Bog-cotton bows to the moorland wind.

The deer's heart skips a beat, he startles.
The sea's tide fills, it rests, it runs.
Season of the drowsy ocean.
Tufts of yellow-blossoming whins.

Bog-banks shine like ravens' wings.
The cuckoo keeps on calling Welcome.
The speckled fish jumps; and the strong
Warrior is up and running.

A little nippy chirpy fellow
Hits the highest note there is;
The lark sings out his clear tidings.
Summer, shimmer, perfect days.

Seamus Heaney

To a Skylark

Hail to thee, blithe Spirit!
Bird thou never wert,
That from heaven, or near it,
Pourest thy full heart
In profuse strains of unpremeditated art.

Higher still and higher
From the earth thou springest
Like a cloud of fire;
The blue deep thou wingest,
And singing still doth soar, and soaring ever singest.

Percy Bysshe Shelley

Skylark

A skein of song unwinds,
one end tied to a blade of grass;
a thread of sound stretching
from meadow to cloud
pulled taut until it snaps:
and the lark, wings folded,
dives after the loose end.

Catherine Benson

Up on the Downs

Up on the Downs,
Up on the Downs,
A skylark flutters
And the fox barks shrill,
Brown rabbit scutters
And the hawk hangs still.
Up on the Downs,
Up on the Downs,
With butterflies
jigging
like
costumed
clowns.

Here in the Hills,
Here in the Hills,
The long grass flashes
And the sky seems vast,
Rock lizard dashes
And a crow flies past.
Here in the Hills,
Here in the Hills,
With bumble bees
buzzing
like
high-speed
drills.

High on the Heath,
High on the Heath,
The slow-worm slithers
And the trees are few,
Field-mouse dithers
And the speedwell's blue.
High on the Heath,
High on the Heath,
Where grasshoppers
chirp
in the
grass
beneath.

Wes Magee

Little Trotty Wagtail

Little trotty wagtail, he went in the rain,
And tittering, tottering sideways he ne'er got straight again,
He stooped to get a worm, and looked up to catch a fly,
And then he flew away ere his feathers they were dry.

Little trotty wagtail, he waddled in the mud,
And left his little footmarks, trample where he would.
He waddled in the water-pudge and waggle went his tail,
And chirrup up his wings to dry upon the garden rail.

Little trotty wagtail, you nimble all about,
And in the dimpling water-pudge you waddle in and out;
Your home is nigh at hand and in the warm pigsty,
So, little Master Wagtail, I'll bid you goodbye.

John Clare

A Boy's Song

Where the pools are bright and deep,
Where the grey trout lies asleep,
Up the river and over the lea,
That's the way for Billy and me.

Where the blackbird sings the latest,
Where the hawthorn blooms the sweetest,
Where the nestlings chirp and flee,
That's the way for Billy and me.

Where the mowers mow the cleanest,
Where the hay lies thick and greenest,
There to track the homeward bee,
That's the way for Billy and me.

Where the hazel bank is steepest,
Where the shadow falls the deepest,
Where the clustering nuts fall free,
That's the way for Billy and me.

Why the boys should drive away
Little sweet maidens from the play,
Or love to banter and fight so well,
That's the thing I never could tell.

But this I know, I love to play
Through the meadow, among the hay;
Up the water and over the lea,
That's the way for Billy and me.

James Hogg

To the Cuckoo

O blithe newcomer! I have heard,
　I hear thee and rejoice.
O cuckoo! shall I call thee bird,
　Or but a wandering voice?

While I am lying on the grass
　They twofold shout I hear;
From hill to hill it seems to pass,
　At once far off and near.

Though babbling only to the vale
　Of sunshine and of flowers,
Thou bringest unto me a tale
　Of visionary hours.

Thrice welcome, darling of the Spring!
　Even yet thou art to me
No bird, but an invisible thing,
　A voice, a mystery;

The same whom in my schoolboy days
   I listened to; that cry
Which made me look a thousand ways
   In bush, and teem and sky.

To seek thee did I often rove
   Through woods and on the green;
And thou wert still a hope, a love;
   Still longed for, never seen.

And I can listen to thee yet;
   Can lie upon the plain
And listen, till I do beget
   That golden time again.

O blessèd bird! the earth we pace
   Again appears to be
An unsubstantial, fairy place;
   That is fit home for thee!

William Wordsworth

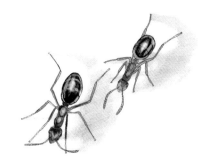

Hopwas Hays Haiku

On a bone dry day
two ants trickle down the hill:
a pair of raindrops

Celia Warren

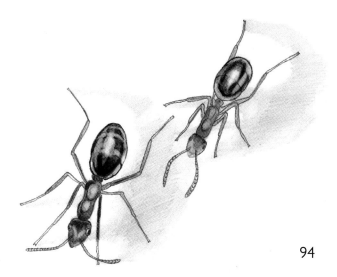

94

Ella's Crane-Flies

Dear Ella, this is a gentle plea
for the daddy-long-legs population
that haunts your room. Don't hoover them up:
let me convert you to conservation.

A dozen years ago I might
have told you they were fairies in disguise,
but now that you're of age I'll say
try seeing them as skinny butterflies.

No? It was never going to work;
phobias aren't susceptible to words.
You'll never love the leggy wisps.
But think of the planet; think of the birds.

Insects are edible, even these
fragile flitters in their gossamer dance.
Let them be hunted; shoo them out
through the open windows to take their chance.

Fleur Adcock

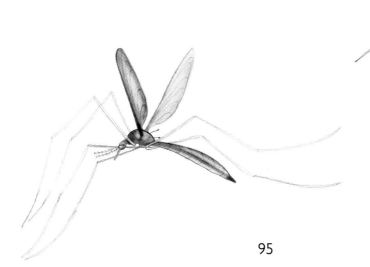

Seeing the Hare

It's in the leap
the joyful hup and hoist on haunches
the paws up fightyaforit
madmarchness of it,
the watchout thumping back feet of it.

The crouch in the grass stillness
the I'm not really here cunning
the longtwitchiness of ears
full of lark song and buzzard's mew
the bony skull full of the distance of it.

Spring fever in its eye holds a magic
a mythology, as if it's come
from some ancient place, offering luck
at seeing it. A once-in-a-blue moon
kind of thing. Getting under your skin.

Catherine Benson

Rabbits

What do rabbits do a lot?
End up in the stewing pot!

That, or flat against the road
(don't they know their Highway Code?);

or they're always on the run,
haring from a hunter's gun.

Lucky then, their foremost habit's
manufacturing more rabbits!

Graham Denton

Slow Worm, Blind Worm, Legless Lizard

In the deep honeyed light of late afternoon a slow worm lies basking,
Her body pulsing to the rhythm of the day; she's at rest.
With lazy lids she blinks, scanning her horizons, always sensitive to changes,
A harmless worm-lizard, giving birth in the cooling September air.
Fuelled by her life's blood, tiny replicas emerge from their secret birth place
And rest in a mangle of copper coils that sparks a dazzle of sunflake gold.
Alarmed out of her reverie, she glides towards the cloaking undergrowth.
Her doll's house versions, thrilling with the newness of life, mimic her reaction
And, like a magician's trick, they all vanish without trace.

Joan McLellan

Aching Bones

There's nothing badder
  than an adder
    with aching bones.
  He moans and groans,
 and hisses and bites
and gets into fights,
  over nothing.
    So something
      has to be done for the adder
    or he becomes badder and madder.
  But teach him some yoga,
he'll sway like a cobra;
  tying himself in knots,
    he'll think sweet thoughts.
      There's nothing gladder
    than an adder
  who owns
flexible bones.

Debjani Chatterjee

Sand Lizard

Tongue teasing the air.
Jade glazed scales flushed to impress,
Poised to mate or flee.

Joan McLellan

Young Adder

A bootlace on my path
  suddenly springs up,
flicks its tongue, assessing me –
  or at least my bike.

Mostly moss green,
  its markings a wave
of jagged black glass
  to warn me off this tiddler

who observes the tyre
  running round my wheel
in a perfect circle –
  like the world seen as a snake

but under the weight
  of an enemy – me,
someone who makes it
  coil unnaturally.

We freeze and wait –
  till it senses victory,
slithers into undergrowth
  and lets me go.

Jill Townsend

Creatures

The butterfly, alive inside a box,
Beats with its powdered wings in soundless knocks
And wishes polythene were hollyhocks.

The beetle clambering across the road
Appears to find his body quite a load:
My fingers meddle with his highway code.

And slugs are rescued from the fatal hiss
Of tyres that kiss like zigzagged liquorice
On zigzagged liquorice, but sometimes miss.

Two snails are raced across a glistening stone,
Each eye thrust forward like a microphone,
So slowly that the winner is unknown.

To all these little creatures I collect,
I mean no cruelty or disrespect,
Although their day-by-day routine is wrecked.

They may remember their experience,
Though at the time it made no sort of sense,
And treat it with a kind of reverence.

It may be something that they never mention,
An episode outside their apprehension,
Like some predestined intervention.

John Fuller

Caterpillar

Brown and furry
Caterpillar in a hurry,
Take your walk
To the shady leaf, or stalk,
Or what not,
Which may be the chosen spot.
No toad spy you,
Hovering bird of prey pass by you;
Spin and die,
To live again a butterfly.

Christina Rossetti

The seven brains of a caterpillar

My first brain thinks the colour of my skin;
Dresses me as green as lettuce.
My second brain arranges crawling;
One slow sucker foot. Hump and wriggle.
Brain three says eat.
Four lullabies me.
Five dreams my breathing;
Lets the wet air suck sweetly in and out.
Six senses danger;
Rolls me up bud-tight at a touch.
But seven lies still. Does nothing. Bides.
It will spin me a shroud, set me my coffin.
Pupa. Pupa. Sound it like a pulse.
From this dead shell I will be born again.
A butterfly. An angel.

Jan Dean

Hoverfly.

Flying Crooked

The butterfly, a cabbage-white,
(His honest idiocy of flight)
Will never now, it is too late,
Master the art of flying straight,
Yet has – who knows so well as I? –
A just sense of how not to fly:
He lurches here and here by guess
And God and hope and hopelessness.
Even the aerobatic swift
Has not his flying-crooked gift.

Robert Graves

Don't Tread on Worms!

I'm asking you nicely:
Please don't tread on worms –
Even though you dislike
All their wriggles and squirms.
You see, there's a great deal
About the earthworm
That deserves your regard
And respect and concern.
First, the tunnels it makes
In the darkness down there
Let into the ground
Both water and air
And it swallows each day
Dead leaves and such stuff
Along with much earth –
It can't get enough!
Then out it all comes
As nice crumbly soil –
Saving the gardener
Much back-breaking toil.
If you think about that
You'll find it confirms
The idea that you shouldn't
Be nasty to worms.

Eric Finney

The Good, the Bad and the Wriggly

Worms Eat My Garbage – a marvellous book;
I keep it beside me whenever I cook.
Whether cabbage or cauliflower, parsnip or pea,
My vermicular family has it for tea.

We should cultivate Nature, for bugs are our mates,
And help us to grow what we put on our plates.
Some relationships thrive but it has to be said:
Although worms eat my garbage, the wasps eat my shed!

You can hear, when it's quiet, the sound of a scraper
As Jasper & Co make their mouth-crafted paper.
Their nest is a bell with a hole in the floor
And it hangs from the roof of the shed, by the door.

They are quiet little wasps, not the frightening things
Who interrupt picnics with buzzes and stings.
They come and they go with a shimmer of gold,
And next year they will build somewhere else, I am told.

My shed is still standing, though roughened in patches,
And I don't mind at all the wasps' nibbles and scratches.
There's room for us all, so I'm coming to terms
With my alien lodgers, the wasps and the worms.

Jane A Russell

The Dragon-fly

Today I saw the dragon-fly
Come from the wells where he did lie.
An inner impulse rent the veil
Of his old husk: from head to tail
Came out clear plates of sapphire mail.
He dried his wings: like gauze they grew;
Thro' crofts and pastures wet with dew
A living flash of light he flew.

Alfred, Lord Tennyson

from To a Butterfly

I've watched you now a full half-hour;
Self-poised upon that yellow flower
And, little Butterfly! indeed
I know not if you sleep or feed.
How motionless! – not frozen seas
More motionless! and then
What joy awaits you, when the breeze
Hath found you out among the trees,
And calls you forth again!

William Wordsworth

There was an Old Man with a Beard

There was an Old Man with a beard,
Who said, 'It is just as I feared! –
    Two Owls and a Hen
    Four Larks and a Wren
Have all built their nests in my beard!'

Edward Lear

There was an Old Man in a Tree

There was an old man in a tree
Who was horribly bored by a bee;
    When they asked, 'Does it buzz?'
    He replied, 'Yes, it does!
It's a regular brute of a bee!'

Edward Lear

Bee! I'm expecting you!

Bee! I'm expecting you!
Was saying Yesterday
To Somebody you know
That you were due –

The Frogs Got Home last Week –
Are settled, and at work –
Birds, mostly back –
The clover warm and thick –

You'll get my Letter by
The seventeenth; Reply
Or Better, be with me –
Yours, Fly.

Emily Dickinson

A Cult Of Bees

Today she rises and she dresses.
Every one of us is her attendant in the robing room –

drone, worker, even the queen.
Every drop squeezed from our bodies, wax and honey,

is to fashion her a body,
a shape in this world, and it glows, as if she was the one

true candle, of which all
your candles are the stray reflections, very far and small.

Today she rises and will be robed
in our wings, spun pearl, which we shed for her gladly,

strew them at her feet like petals.
We lay out our bodies, scattered on the orchard floor,

swept out of doors of the hive.
We are her feelers, glands and limbs. We have no word

for what we, each by each,
might be, as ready for the journey now she rises,

and we clothe her with ourselves.
She is nothing, and all that we are: the ungraspable pattern

in the live brocade of swarming,
the shapes that we trace in the air, always threading our amber

beads on their string. She
is… But ask your candle, in its whispering under the breath

of the flame. She cares
for everything, and cares for nothing. She is not for you.

Philip Gross

Ant Number 1,049,652

Like a small yacht over a sea of grass
He tacks, carrying a green sail of leaf.

On the goad of his own acid he hastes
To receive or bestow a merciless death.

War machine directed by an unseen commander,
Minute mobile bottle of lethal chemical.

His mind lies outside his body. He is a fury
Of unbending purpose. The leaf will be delivered.

Gerard Benson

Earwig

Forward, the earwig!
Antennae salute,
Pincer movement
Brings up the rear.
Keep the barrel well polished,
Never know when you might need it,
On dry dahlia stalking.

Regimental legs tattoo
To winter quarters,
Until
        Quick March.

David Orme

Woodlouse

Armoured dinosaur,
blundering through jungle grass by
dandelion-light.

Knight's headpiece, steel-hinged
orange-segment, ball-bearing,
armadillo-drop.

Pale peppercorn, pearled
eyeball; sentence without end,
my rolling full-stop.

Judith Nicholls

A Goldfinch

This feather-soft creature
Tail to head,
Is golden yellow,
And black, and red.

A sip of water,
A twig to sit on,
A prong for a nest,
The air to wing on.

A mate to love,
Some thistledown seed
Are all his joy, life,
Beauty, need.

Walter de la Mare

Bullfinch

Suddenly, from yew
to bursting branch
a bright blur of breast feathers
a startle of white rump.
He is a flying peach
round as a rosy tennis ball
on the branch he nods and dips.
Nips in the bud
the promise of cherries.

Jan Dean

Tall Nettles

Tall nettles cover up, as they have done
These many springs, the rusty harrow, the plough
Long worn out, and the roller made of stone:
Only the elm butt tops the nettles now.

This corner of the farmyard I like most:
As well as any bloom upon a flower
I like the dust on the nettles, never lost
Except to prove the sweetness of a shower.

Edward Thomas

On the Grasshopper and the Cricket

The poetry of earth is never dead:
　　When all the birds are faint with the hot sun,
　　And hide in cooling trees, a voice will run
From hedge to hedge about the new-mown mead;
That is the Grasshopper's – he takes the lead
　　In summer luxury – he has never done
　　With his delights; for when tired out with fun
He rests at ease beneath some pleasant weed.
The poetry of earth is ceasing never:
　　On a lone winter evening, when the frost
　　Has wrought a silence, from the stove there shrills
The Cricket's song, in warmth increasing ever,
　　And seems to one in drowsiness half lost,
　　The Grasshopper's among some grassy hills.

John Keats

10/10/01   Pitton. Wood. Farm.   ♂ Southern Hawker Daniel Barritt

River

Dragonflies snatch at light,
spin it into colour.
Hover above water,
reflecting the spectrum.
Rippled glow,
stonesplash gurgle,
spilling downstream,
swallowing light
as wings carry them off –
blue-green specks in the wind.

Rupert M Loydell

120

Summer Paddling

Twee-wee-wee is the sandpiper's song,
With his slender beak and his legs so long.
His reflection shivers on the water's skin
As he wades on legs knobble-kneed thin.

He bobs his head; he bobs his tail,
Paddling and probing a mud-covered snail.
In mountain loch he struts and pokes,
Muddying water with weed-bed smoke.

Twee-wee-wee is the sandpiper's song,
Intruder wary, all summer long.
Green-brown blending among the reeds,
Little stilt-walker of summer's first breeze.

Coral Rumble

Dancer

In a hollow tree the otter sits –
Wire whiskers twitching,
Head held still in ballerina pose,
Listening for the rustle of a hunter's walk,
For the splash of a stone from passing boys,
For an alien call from hungry lips.
His thick, brown fur trembles,
His body shudders from flattened head
To tapered tail.
Webbed feet root to the spot.
But when the dusk has settled,
And night-time calls meet his own
Thin, high-pitched whistle,
River reeds part
And the dancer slides
Into underwater steps
And a pirouette of bubbles.

Coral Rumble

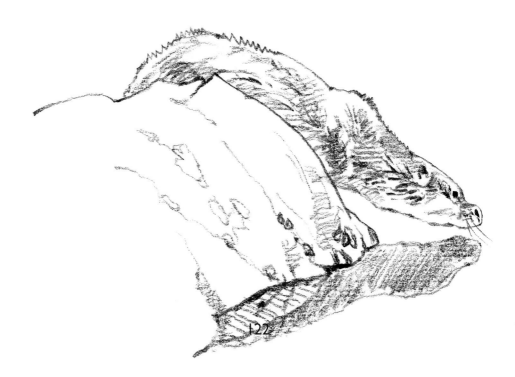

Salmon says ...

How little you use your senses
Though you think yourselves so advanced!
Have you savoured the waves of the ocean
For the flavour of your first dance?
Have you traced the taste through reeking deeps
To the waters where you were born?
We have swum thousands of briny miles
To leap upstream to spawn.

And now we are proud of our offspring.
They will dance their parents' dance.
They, too, will follow the scent back home,
We salmon leave nothing to chance.
Poor you, with your cars and ships and planes;
Your rockets that fly to the moon!
You can't even smell or taste your way
To yesterday afternoon!

Celia Warren

The Wild Swans At Coole

The trees are in their autumn beauty,
The woodland paths are dry,
Under the October twilight the water
Mirrors a still sky;
Upon the brimming water among the stones
Are nine-and-fifty Swans.
The nineteenth autumn has come upon me
Since I first made my count;
I saw, before I had well finished,
All suddenly mount
And scatter wheeling in great broken rings
Upon their clamorous wings.
I have looked upon those brilliant creatures,
And now my heart is sore.

All's changed since I, hearing at twilight,
The first time on this shore,
The bell-beat of their wings above my head,
Trod with a lighter tread.
Unwearied still, lover by lover,
They paddle in the cold
Companionable streams or climb the air;
Their hearts have not grown old;
Passion or conquest, wander where they will,
Attend upon them still.
But now they drift on the still water,
Mysterious, beautiful;
Among what rushes will they build,
By what lake's edge or pool
Delight men's eyes when I awake some day
To find they have flown away?

WB Yeats

125

The Eagle

He clasps the crag with crooked hands;
Close to the sun in lonely lands,
Ringed with the azure world, he stands.

The wrinkled sea beneath him crawls;
He watches from his mountain walls,
And like a thunderbolt he falls.

Alfred, Lord Tennyson

Kestrel

Slide the sky
switch to hover
fast-jet silhouette
defies the laws of aviation
tricks the wind
fifteen metres vertical
tic left, tuck right, spread

killer profile
aileron   rudder   fan
not engineered, no drilled stainless steel
or pinions in titanium
no carbon fibre struts –
ten months ago
this was an egg

jink sidelong at hint of scamper
raptor fixed against the gale
instinctive autopilot
feather tips on gyro duty
tracking focus…

drop-six-metres-stop
quick as that
undercarriage folded, fix…

stoop
flurry
kill

Ian Royce Chamberlain

Crab

In the low tide pools
I pack myself like
A handy pocket
Chest of tools.

But as the tide fills
Dancing I go
Under lifted veils
Tiptoe, tiptoe.

And with pliers and pincers
Repair and remake
The daintier dancers
The breakers break.

Ted Hughes

128

Nuffin' Like a Puffin

Rockin' around the clock of an island,
on the high wire of an Atlantic gale:
with shambling wingbeats
to hold up a body that's
as tubby, as stubby and as chubby
as an April aubergine.
With that clown's coulterneb*
and evening wear,
these top-billing Chaplins
are as angelic, as iconic, as innocent
as the master himself.
Elegant amid gannets, pirate skuas
and icy feathered terns,
the puffin flight is as round as a rose.
The landing, though, is unsure
a rolling, looping pull-out
as the seacliff looms.
Mind you, after seven months at sea,
these dicey aeronautics are no surprise.
Home is this island riddled with tunnels,
honeycombed with burrows,
strewn with nests where these colourful tenants
feed their dumpy, plumpy pufflings.
Puffin, gawky when airbound,
sleek under water like seals.

John Rice

*coulterneb – a Scottish word meaning beak as keen as a blade

(Unbridled) Guillemot

I'm a guillemot
I use my skill a lot
I get the fish out of the wet
I eat my fill a lot.
I live on ledges
vertical edges
eating-wise, I do not know what veg is
Don't give me sherbet
give me a turbot
my appetite for fish I cannot curb it.
Here's lines more in the manner of George Herbert:

      The fish, it swimmeth, unaware

      and, rumbled, down I tumble to my prey,

      to pluck it forth, my instinct, I obey,

      from water to the stifling air,

      I'll whip the little whipper-snap away.

I'm a guillemot,
so you don't thrill a lot?
Well, listen humans, very soon you will a lot.
Did you know that I can go so deep
I've been seen from the porthole of a submerged submarine,
sixty meters under?
I don't think so.
Miss it and blink so
I come in hard and I'm able to sink so.
I'm a guillemot
I know the drill a lot
I drill into the drink and get the drink and not the ink upon my quill a lot.
I don't do nesting,
when I'm resting
I can sleep while I am standing on one leg,
and so it doesn't roll off

when I stretch my wings or stroll off
I've got an egg that's eccentrically weighted so it rolls around in circles
and doesn't fall over the edge of the cliff.
I do my perchin
and my researchin
then underneath I go.
I'm no sea-urchin
I'm a guillemot
I do my speccy reccy from my rocky window sill a lot
I am homeless
but I'm not gormless,
I can go so quick it's almost like I'm formless
I'm a guillemot
I find the fishes tend to lose one-nil a lot,
but I take only what I need
I'm not a greedy bird.
I am sustainable.
Self restrainable.
I am a guillemot.
I don't eat Trill a lot.
I'm a guillemot.
Am I not?

John Hegley

Bird Raptures

The sunrise wakes the lark to sing,
The moonrise wakes the nightingale.
Come darkness, moonrise, everything
That is so silent, sweet, and pale,
Come, so ye wake the nightingale.

Make haste to mount, thou wistful moon,
Make haste to wake the nightingale:
Let silence set the world in tune
To hearken to that wordless tale
Which warbles from the nightingale.

Christina Rossetti

Mushrooms

The night before, a great moon full of honey
Had flowed up behind the hills and poured across the fields.

The leaves were rustling, the wheat whispered
Dry and gold in the wind's hands.

Andrew and I went to Foss. We drove over hills
That were blustery with huge gusts of sunlight.

We stopped and walked to the loch, left two trails
Through the grass, came on the mushrooms by accident,

A village of strewn white hats,
The folds of their gills underneath as soft as skin.

We almost did not want to take them, as if
It would be theft – wronging the hills, the trees, the grass.

But in the end we did, we picked them with reverence;
And they broke like bread between our hands, we carried whole armfuls home,

Pieces of field, smelling of earth and autumn;
A thanksgiving, a blessing.

Kenneth C Steven

133

Proud Songsters

The thrushes sing as the sun is going,
And the finches whistle in ones and pairs,
And as it gets dark loud nightingales
In bushes
Pipe, as they can when April wears,
As if all Time were theirs.

These are brand-new birds of twelve-months' growing,
Which a year ago, or less than twain,
No finches were, nor nightingales,
Nor thrushes,
But only particles of grain,
And earth, and air, and rain.

Thomas Hardy

Heron

Before footfall disturbs dew,
bamboo flickers and susurrates.
The lawn is spotted with apples,
wormy windfalls, bruised and tart.
The rock garden wears
pink and blue stitchery.

Suddenly, like an apparition,
landing, come to steal,
wading into the fish pond,
a bold heron. His grace,
for one moment, astonishes,

before we bang on windows,
disturb his breakfast. Barely
acknowledging us, he rises,
nonchalant. Lucifer
flying back to heaven,
beautiful as sin.

Angela Topping

Take off

Rough stubble glows, burnt apricot.
A buzzard soars. Light clings.
His breast a travelling sunset,
He warms the world with wings.

Alison Brackenbury

Bedtime

The evening is coming,
    The sun sinks to rest;
The rooks are all flying
    Straight home to their nest,
"Caw!" says the rook, as he flies overhead,
"It's time little people were going to bed!"

The flowers are closing;
    The daisy's asleep,
The primrose is buried
    In slumber so deep.
Shut up for the night is the pimpernel red;
It's time little people were going to bed!

The butterfly drowsy
    Has folded its wing;
The bees are returning,
    No more the birds sing.
Their labour is over, their nestlings are fed;
It's time little people were going to bed!

Here comes the pony,
    His work is all done;
Down through the meadow
    he takes a good run;
Up go his heels, and down goes his head;
It's time little people were going to bed!

Good night, little people,
    Good night and good night;
Sweet dreams to your eyelids
    Till dawning of light;
The evening has come, there's no more to be said,
It's time little people were going to bed!

Thomas Hood

137

Shadow

Across my bedroom wall
flapping its giant wings:
A monster.

Across my bedroom lamp
fluttering its small brown wings:
a moth.

Michael Rosen

138

The Centipede

I objurgate the centipede,
A bug we do not really need.
At sleepy-time he beats a path
Straight to the bedroom or the bath.
You always wallop where's he's not,
Or, if he is, he makes a spot.

Ogden Nash

The Firefly

The firefly is a funny bug,
He hasn't any mind;
He blunders all the way through life
With his headlight on behind.

Anonymous

Mice

I think mice
Are rather nice.

Their tails are long,
Their faces small,
They haven't any
Chins at all.
Their ears are pink,
Their teeth are white,
They run about
The house at night.
They nibble things
They shouldn't touch
And no one seems
To like them much.

But I think mice
Are nice.

Rose Fyleman

Field Mouse Sleeping

Beneath the moon
beneath the corn
mouse is sleeping
maybe dreaming

off and on
of better things
like limbs with wings
like ears for eyes

to rise up into
big black skies
to loop around
to see in sound

be careful where
you do your creeping
mouse is sleeping
maybe dreaming

James Carter

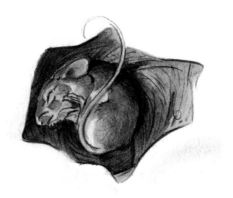

Floating Harbour

On the same posts each evening
the harbour cormorants
hang out their wings to dry
like the day's umbrellas
as the late ferry passes.

In sour-sweet ramparts of ivy
the blackbirds call
drowsily, piercingly.
Above them the gulls
are casing the terraces.

Thickly, the pigeons
groom their own voices
as parents in the half-light
tiptoe away from babies
over their heads in sleep.

Helen Dunmore

Blue Herons

One swoops in on a glider wing
Two stick-picks the shore

Three stands stiff as a soldier boy
Waiting for soldier four

Five parades in his downy coat
Six inspects a toad

Seven leans into a singing wind
Eight's on the river road

Nine flies up to the bird-bent tree
Ten wears a midnight plume

Eleven talks back to the gossipy wren
Twelve's in his watery room

J Patrick Lewis

Cliché

They came between dusk blue
and the watery moon's rising,
arrows of geese
that made the sky a river
flecked with froth.

Their calling silvered the air,
reflected in glass and puddles,
made twilight a cliché.

But one small boy
who knew geese only from a picture book
watched,
gasped,
wondered.

Alison Chisholm

Something Told the Wild Geese

Something told the wild geese
It was time to go.
Though the fields lay golden
Something whispered – 'Snow'.
Leaves were green and stirring,
Berries, lustre-glossed,
But beneath warm feathers
Something cautioned – 'Frost'.

All the sagging orchards
Steamed with amber spice,
But each wild breast stiffened
At remembered ice.
Something told the wild geese
It was time to fly –
Summer sun was on their wings,
Winter in their cry.

Rachel Field

Bat

Little mouse with leathern wings,
inaudible, so high it sings.

A twilight swoop, a dusky flitter,
a shadow-glimpse, a hint of twitter.

In barn or tower, or loft in town,
you'll find it hanging upside down.

Cahoots with owl and crone and cat,
a swirly, looping, spooking ... bat.

Tony Mitton

Bat Words

Why do people
get tightup,
because we here
hang downside up?

Are scared they of
our bat wings black?
Or of our knees
on front to back?

We're bottom up,
but don't please fuss –
for you're the way
round wrong to us!

Liz Brownlee

The Owl

When cats run home and light is come,
　And dew is cold upon the ground,
And the far-off stream is dumb,
　And the whirring sail goes round,
　And the whirring sail goes round;
　　Alone and warming his five wits,
　　The white owl in the belfry sits.

When merry milkmaids click the latch,
　And rarely smells the new mown hay,
And the cock hath sung beneath the thatch
　Twice or thrice his roundelay,
　Twice or thrice his roundelay;
　　Alone and warming his five wits,
　　The white owl in the belfry sits.

Alfred, Lord Tennyson

Night Hunter

All must be still when the barn owl flies,
Whiskers and feet and tails!
Watch for the mask with the round bright eyes
And the wings like great white sails.

All will be well when the barn owl glides
Back to his high dark den.
Wise is the vole or shrew that hides
When his cry is heard again!

Sue Cowling

Riddle

Like a small Bear it
bundles over the dArk road,
brushes past the front gate,
as if she owns the joint.
rolls the Dustbin
like an expert barrel rider.
Tucks into yesterday's Garbage,
crunches worms for titbits.
Wakes us from deep slEep,
blinks back at torchlight.
Our midnight feasteR,
ghost-friend,
moon-lit,
zebra bear.

Pie Corbett

Badger

Through the trees I saw a badger
Early evening, nearly dusk
All the midges dancing round me
Foxglove scent, and ferny musk.

Through the trees I saw a badger
In the twilight, stars just out
Bats like rags were drifting, swooping
Sheep on hillside, farmer's shout.

Through the trees I saw a badger
Through the air as grey as smoke
Light as dancers she came listening
Light as ghosts she sniffed the dark.

Through the trees I saw a badger
Barred head lifted, wary, keen,
Then she faded through the bracken
Like a whisper, like a dream.

Berlie Doherty

Index of Titles

Aching Bones *Debjani Chatterjee* 99
All Creatures *Gervase Phinn* 83
Ant Number 1,049,652
  Gerard Benson 114
Araneus Diadematus *Gerard Benson* 78
Arion Ater Agg: The Black Slug
  Paul Hughes 34
As the Osprey to the Fish
  Andrew Motion 4

Badger *Berlie Doherty* 151
Bat *Tony Mitton* 146
Bat Words *Liz Brownlee* 147
Bedtime *Thomas Hood* 137
Bee! I'm expecting you!
  Emily Dickinson 111
Bird at Dawn, The *Harold Monro* 42
Bird came down the Walk, A
  Emily Dickinson 63
Bird Raptures *Christina Rossetti* 132
Blackberry, The *Rory Ewins* 80
Black Swan *Graham Burchell* 41
Blue Herons *J Patrick Lewis* 143
Boy's Song, A *James Hogg* 91
Brief Reflection on Cats Growing in Trees
  Miroslav Holub 58
Broken Morning *Moira Andrew* 16
Bullfinch *Jan Dean* 117

Caterpillar *Christina Rossetti* 103
Centipede, The *Ogden Nash* 139
from Child's Song in Spring *E Nesbit* 24
City Bees *Jennifer Curry* 49
Cliché *Alison Chisholm* 144
Conker *Judith Nicholls* 81
Crab *Ted Hughes* 128
Creatures *John Fuller* 102
Crow *Roger Stevens* 50

Cult Of Bees, A *Philip Gross* 112
Cut Grass *Philip Larkin* 53

Dancer *Coral Rumble* 122
Dipper, The *Kathleen Jamie* 17
Don't Tread on Worms! *Eric Finney* 106
Down the Stream the Swans all Glide
  Spike Milligan 40
Dragon-fly, The *Alfred, Lord Tennyson* 108
Ducks' Ditty *Kenneth Grahame* 39

Eagle, The *Alfred, Lord Tennyson* 126
Earwig *David Orme* 114
Ella's Crane-Flies *Fleur Adcock* 95

Field Mouse Sleeping *James Carter* 141
Firefly, The *Anonymous* 139
First Day, The *Phoebe Hesketh* 10
Floating Harbour *Helen Dunmore* 142
Flying Crooked *Robert Grave* 105
Fly, The *William Blake* 82
Forest End *Judith Nicholls* 37
Foxgloves *Jill Townsend* 80
Frog Hop *John Agard* 44

Gardener's Song, The *Gareth Owen* 54
from Glanmore Eclogue
  Seamus Heaney 86
Goldfinch, A *Walter de la Mare* 117
Good, the Bad and the Wriggly, The
  Jane A Russell 107
Gorse *Gerard Benson* 68
Green Stink, A *Gerard Benson* 73

Haiku *Alison Hunt* 12
Haiku *J W Hackett* 13
Hedgehog *Liz Brownlee* 55
Heron *Angela Topping* 135
Home-Thoughts, from Abroad
  Robert Browning 65
Hopwas Hays Haiku *Celia Warren* 94

Irony *WH Hudson* 71
from The Ivy Green *Charles Dickens* 36
I Wish I Was a Bird *Roger Stevens* 14

Jenny Wren *Walter de la Mare* 62

Kestrel *Ian Royce Chamberlain* 127

Ladette *Alison Chisholm* 72
Ladybird! Ladybird! *Emily Brontë* 85
Little Trotty Wagtail *John Clare* 90
London Sparrows *Philip Waddell* 66
Loveliest of Trees *A E Housman* 23

Mayfly, The *Andrew Collett* 70
Mice *Rose Fyleman* 140
Mole *Liz Brownlee* 56
Moor-Hens *Charles Causley* 38
Mr Snail *Celia Warren* 35
Mushrooms *Kenneth C Steven* 133

Nature Trail *Benjamin Zephaniah* 32
Night Hunter *Sue Cowling* 149
Night Prowler *Jennifer Curry* 61
No Hurry *Eric Finney* 75
Nothing Grows Old *Phoebe Hesketh* 64
Nuffin' Like a Puffin *John Rice* 129

Ode by a Nightingale *Rory Ewins* 43
Old Foxy *Sue Hardy-Dawson* 60
On the Grasshopper and the Cricket
  John Keats 119
Owl, The *Alfred, Lord Tennyson* 148

Pippa's Song *Robert Browning* 21
Proud Songsters *Thomas Hardy* 134

Rabbits *Graham Denton* 97
Riddle *Pie Corbett* 150
River *Rupert M Loydell* 120
Robin *Iain Crichton Smith* 15

Rush Hour *Celia Warren* 74

Salmon says … *Celia Warren* 123
Sand Lizard *Joan McLellan* 100
Seeing the Hare *Catherine Benson* 96
Seven brains of a caterpillar, The
  Jan Dean 104
Shadow *Michael Rosen* 138
Shell Villanelle *Tony Mitton* 31
Short Measures *Ben Jonson* 70
Skylark *Catherine Benson* 88
Slow Worm, Blind Worm, Legless Lizard
  Joan McLellan 98
Small, Smaller *Russell Hoban* 18
Snail, The *William Cowper* 30
Something Told the Wild Geese
  Rachel Field 145
Spinner *Alison Brackenbury* 79
from Spring *Christina Rossetti* 20
Squirrel's the Word *Sophie Hannah* 29
Stick-Insect, A *Brian Moses* 84
Summer Paddling *Coral Rumble* 121

Tadpoles *Peter Dixon* 46
Take off *Alison Brackenbury* 136
Tall Nettles *Edward Thomas* 118
Thaw *Edward Thomas* 19
There was an Old Man with a Beard
  Edward Lear 110
There was an Old Man in a Tree
  Edward Lear 110
Thistle *Philip Waddell* 69
Thrush's Nest, The *John Clare* 28
Tiding of Magpies, A *Cornelia Davies* 51
from To a Butterfly
  William Wordsworth 109
Toad *Norman MacCaig* 45
To a Skylark *Percy Bysshe Shelley* 87
To the Cuckoo *William Wordsworth* 92
Trees *Sara Coleridge* 22
Trees, The *Graham Corcoran* 26

Twenty Minute Walk *Angela France* 48

(Unbridled) Guillemot *John Hegley* 130
Up on the Downs *Wes Magee* 89

Very Fortunate Frog, The
  Chrissie Gittins 47

Web of Life *Jane Clarke* 25
Weasel *Ted Hughes* 57
Wild Swans At Coole, The *WB Yeats* 124

Windhover, The
  Gerard Manley Hopkins 52
Woodlouse *Judith Nicholls* 115
Worm's Eye View of the FA Cup Final
  Tony Mitton 76
Worth of Earthworms, The
  Tony Mitton 77
Wren *Celia Warren* 67

Young Adder *Jill Townsend* 101

Acknowledgements

All poems within copyright appear by the kind permission of the copyright holder and may not be reproduced without permission.

'Aching Bones' by Debjani Chatterjee first appeared in *Animal Antics* by Debjani Chatterjee, Pennine Pens, 2000.

'Ant Number 1,049,652' by Gerard Benson first appeared in *To Catch an Elephant, poems by Gerard Benson*, Smith/Doorstop, 2002.

'Araneus Diadematus' by Gerard Benson first appeared in *The Magnificent Callisto* by Gerard Benson, Blackie/Puffin, 1992.

'As the Osprey to the Fish' by Andrew Motion by permission of the author.

'Badger' by Berlie Doherty first appeared in *Walking on Air*, Lions, 1993.

'Bat' by Tony Mitton by permission of the author.

'Bat Words' by Liz Brownlee first published 2007, at Bristol Zoo.

'Brief Reflections on Cats Growing in Trees' by Miroslav Holub first appeared in *Poems Before & After: Collected English Translations*, translated from the Czech by Ian & Jarmila Milner, Ewald Osers, George Theiner, David Young, Dana Hábová, Rebekah Bloyd and Miroslav Holub, Bloodaxe Books, 2006.

'Broken Morning' by Moira Andrew first appeared in *Light the Blue Touch Paper*, Iron Press, 1986.

'Bullfinch' copyright © Jan Dean.

'The Centipede' by Ogden Nash first appeared in The Saturday Evening Post, 1935. Copyright © 1935 by Ogden Nash. Reprinted by permission of Curtis Brown, Ltd.

'City Bees' by Jennifer Curry, from *Down Our Street* by Jennifer and Graeme Curry, Methuen Children's Books, 1988. Copyright © Jennifer Curry.

'Cliché' by Alison Chisholm first appeared in *Mapping the Maze*, Headland Publications, 2004.

'Conker' copyright © Judith Nicholls 2010, reproduced by permission of the author.

the Literary Representative of the Estate of Rose Fyleman.

'Moor-hens' by Charles Causley first appeared in *Collected Poems for Children*.

'Mushrooms' by Kenneth C Steven is reproduced by permission of the author.

'Night Hunter' by Sue Cowling is reproduced by permission of the author.

'Night Prowler' by Jennifer Curry, from *Down Our Street* by Jennifer and Graeme Curry, Methuen Children's Books, 1988. Copyright © Jennifer Curry.

'No Hurry' by Eric Finney first appeared in *Another Fifth Poetry Book* compiled by John Foster, Oxford University Press, 1989.

'Nuffin' Like a Puffin' copyright © John Rice by permission of the author.

'Salmon Says' by Celia Warren first appeared in *Elephants Can't Jump* compiled by Brian Moses, Belitha Press, 2001.

'Seeing The Hare' by Catherine Benson by permission of the author

'The Seven Brains of the Caterpillar' by Jan Dean first published in *Nearly Thirteen*, Blackie, 1995.

'Shadow' from *Centrally Heated Knickers* by Michael Rosen (copyright © Michael Rosen 2000) is reproduced by permission of PFD on behalf of Michael Rosen.

'Shell Villanelle' by Tony Mitton, first published in *The Unidentified Frying Omelette*, compiled by Andrew Fusek Peters, Hodder Wayland, 2000

'Skylark' by Catherine Benson by permission of the author

'Small, Smaller' by Russell Hoban first appeared in *From Poems Selected by Michael Harrison and Christopher Stuart-Clark*, OUP, 1979.

'Spinner' by Alison Brackenbury first appeared in *Selected Poems*, Carcanet.

'Squirrel's The Word' by Sophie Hannah first appeared in *First of the Last Chances*, Carcanet.

'A Stick Insect' by Brian Moses first published in *I Wish I Could Dine With A Porcupine - Poems by Brian Moses*, Hodder Wayland 2000, © Brian Moses.

'Summer Paddling' by Coral Rumble first appeared in *My Teacher's as Wild as a Bison*, Lion Hudson, 2005.

'Thistle' by Philip Waddell, reproduced by permission of the author.

Artists

All art is copyright © the artist, as listed below, and may not be reproduced without permission:

Carry Akroyd (www.carryakroyd.co.uk): back cover, 24–5, 30–1, 56–7, 64–5, 70–1, 96–7, 106–7, 136–7

David Bennett (www.davidbennettwildlifeart.moonfruit.com): 16–17, 104–5, 108–9, 120–1, 128–9

John Busby: 5, 10, 14–15, 18–19, 38–9, 50–1, 62–3, 66–7, 86–7, 90–1, 122–3, 126–7, 134–5

John Davis: 150–1

Brin Edwards (www.brin-edwards.com): 116

John Edwards: 43, 54–5, 98

Helen Hanson (www.helenhanson.co.uk): 88–9, 92–3

Richard Lewington (www.richardlewington.co.uk): 78–9, 102–3, 114–5

Sean Longcroft (www.longcroft.net): 26–7, 34–5, 46–7, 58–9, 76–7, 110–1, 131, 138–9

James McCallum (www.jamesmccallum.co.uk): 1, 124–5, 144–5

John Norris Wood: 44–5, 84–5

Jane Leycester Paige (www.oldbrewerystudios.co.uk): 36–7, 68–9, 72–3

John Paige (www.oldbrewerystudios.co.uk): front cover, 12–13

Peter Partington (www.peter-partington.fsnet.co.uk): 28–9, 32–3, 52–3, 61, 74–5, 132–3, 140–1

Greg Poole (www.gregpoole.co.uk): 20–1, 142–3

Dan Powell: 100–1

Martin Ridley (www.martinridley.com): 148–9

Andrew Tyzack (www.thelandgallery.com): 82–3, 94–5, 112–3

Sue Vise: 22–3, 48–9, 80–1, 118–9

Mike Warren (www.mikewarren.co.uk): 40–1

With thanks to:

Andrew Tyzack of the Land Gallery, who has been extraordinarily helpful in sourcing the artwork as well as contributing beautiful images of his own.

Dr Mark Boyd of the RSPB for his generously given expertise.

Kate Paice and Rachel Kellehar of A&C Black for their enthusiasm, hard work and support.